Maria Linnemann

My Beautiful Country

15 leichte Stücke für Gitarre

15 easy pieces for guitar

Sy. 2885

RICORDI

This new collection of solo pieces once more reflects the many sources of inspiration that I have encountered on my travels around the world in past decades. I hope they afford much pleasure to all whose fingers bring them to life.

Maria Linnemann

Diese neue Sammlung von Solostücken spiegelt einmal mehr die vielen Inspirations-quellen wieder, die mir in den vergangenen Jahrzehnten auf meinen Reisen um die Welt begegnet sind. Ich hoffe, sie bereiten allen, deren Finger sie zum Leben erwecken, viel Freude!

Maria Linnemann

für Ingrid

Chant de Haute-Provence

Maria Linnemann

Edition Ricordi

Sy. 2885

für Bea

Wallflower

Maria Linnemann

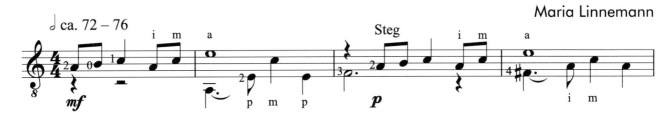

Edition Ricordi   Sy. 2885   © 2012 by G. Ricordi & Co.

für Victor

Traffic Jam Blues

Maria Linnemann

a tempo

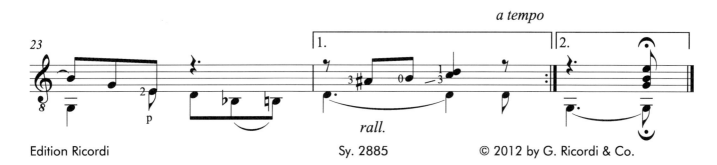

Edition Ricordi Sy. 2885

für Tirke

Lullaby for a Violin

Maria Linnemann

Sy. 2885

poco rall.

a tempo

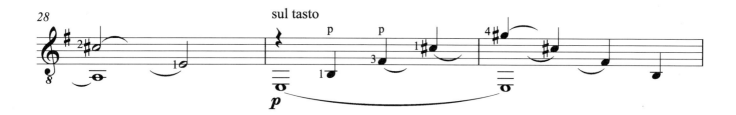

sul tasto

loco

Da Capo
al

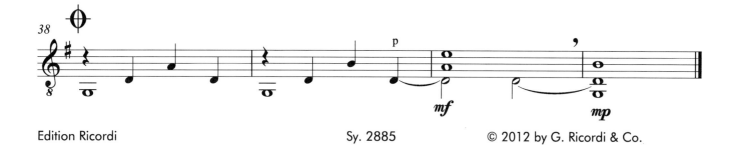

für Harald

Kopfstand-Rumba

Lebhaft / Lively

♩ ca.152 – 184

Maria Linnemann

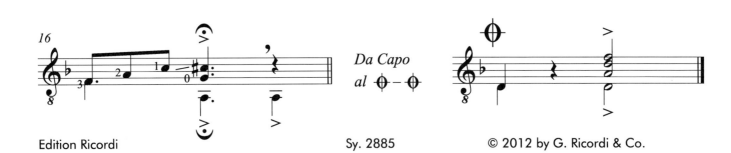

Edition Ricordi

Sy. 2885

für Christian

Prelude

Maria Linnemann

Espressivo

♩ ca. 96 – 112

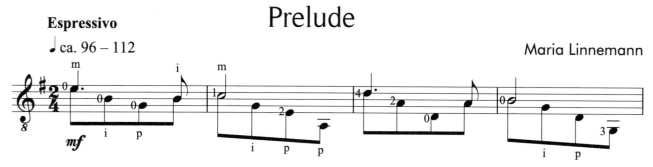

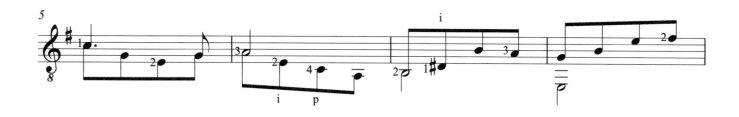

poco rall.

Edition Ricordi

Sy. 2885

Da Svidanya

Maria Linnemann

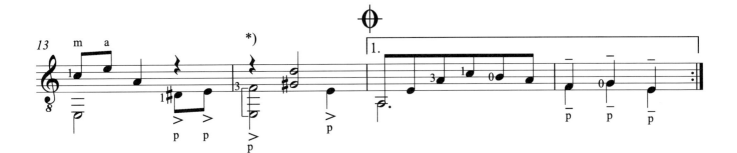

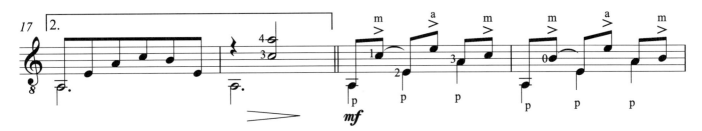

*) Der Daumen schlägt kurz vor dem Schlag *E* an, danach auf den Schlag *f*. Die 5. Saite wird dabei übersprungen.
The thumb plucks the note E *shortly before the beat and then* f *on the beat. The 5th string is passed over.*

Edition Ricordi
Sy. 2885

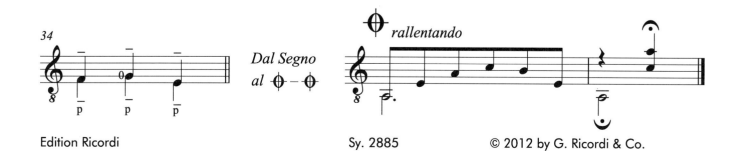

Edition Ricordi

Sy. 2885

für Philip

Take-It-Easy-Blues

Langsam und lässig / Slow and nonchalant

Maria Linnemann

♩. ca. 80 – 86

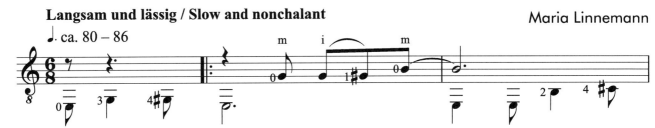

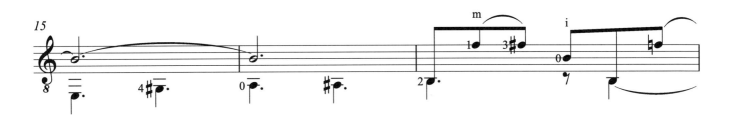

Edition Ricordi

Sy. 2885

© 2012 by G. Ricordi & Co.

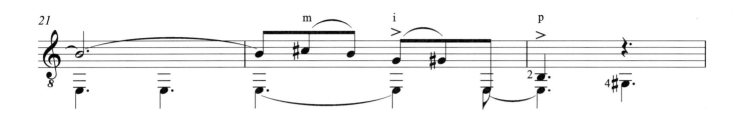

molto rallentando

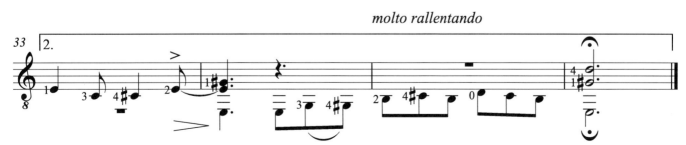

*) Das *cis* entsteht durch Aufschlagen des vierten Fingers auf die 5. Saite.
   Play c-sharp *by striking the 5th string with the 4th finger.*

Edition Ricordi   Sy. 2885   © 2012 by G. Ricordi & Co.

Do You Remember?
(Tango)

Maria Linnemann

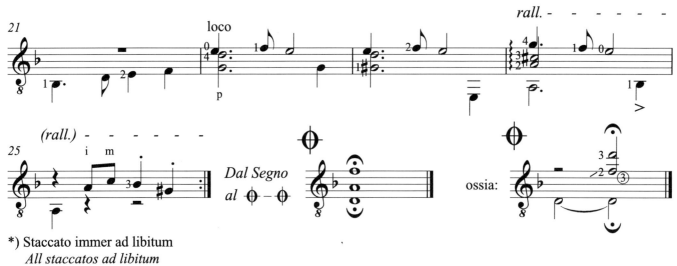

*) Staccato immer ad libitum
All staccatos ad libitum

Edition Ricordi   Sy. 2885   © 2012 by G. Ricordi & Co.

Without a Care

(Jig)

Maria Linnemann

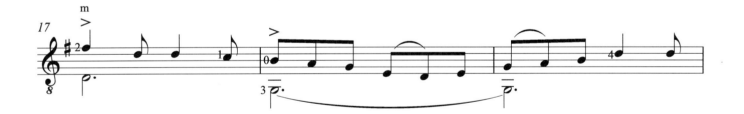

Edition Ricordi

Sy. 2885

für Philip

Masha's Waltz

Maria Linnemann

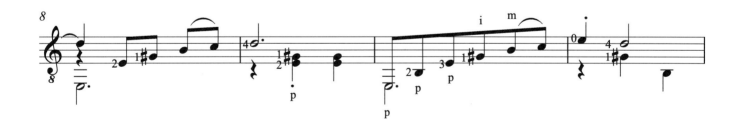

Sy. 2885

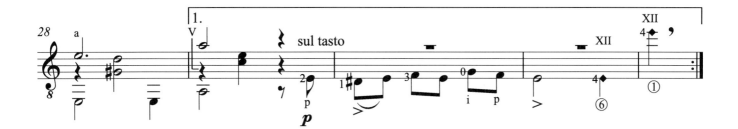

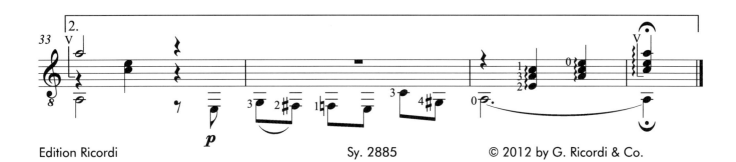

für Eva

Serendipity

Meditativ / Meditatively

♩ ca. 84 – 92

Maria Linnemann

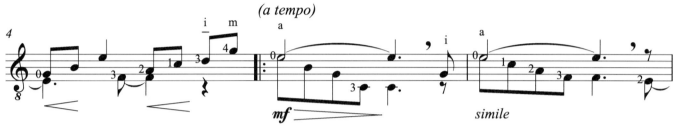

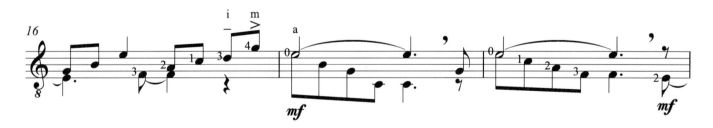

Edition Ricordi

Sy. 2885

für Sabine

My Beautiful Country

Maria Linnemann

Edition Ricordi　　　　　Sy. 2885

für Victor

Rhythm Section

Maria Linnemann

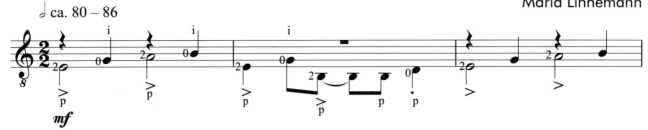

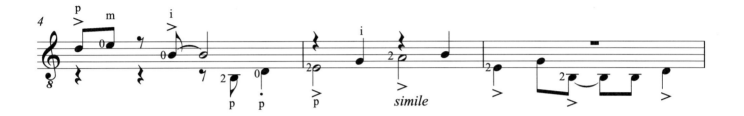

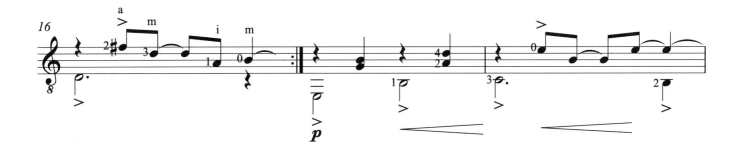

*) Wenn ad-libitum-Abschnitt (Takt 25-28) nicht gespielt wird: Direkt nach Takt 24 *Da Capo al* ⊕ – ⊕ spielen.
If the ad libitum section (bar 25-28) is not played: Da Capo al ⊕ – ⊕ directly after bar 24.

Edition Ricordi   Sy. 2885   © 2012 by G. Ricordi & Co.

Tango en las sombras

(Hommage à A. P.)

Maria Linnemann

Edition Ricordi

Sy. 2885

*) Künstliches Flageolett: Linke Hand greift wie gewohnt; **i** berührt die Saite über dem bezeichneten Bundstab
(jeweils eine Oktave höher als die geschriebene Note); **a** schlägt an, **i** gibt die Saite unmittelbar nach dem
Anschlag frei.

*Artificial flageolet: Left hand plays as usual; **i** lightly touches the string on top of the fret indicated (always one
octave higher than the written note); **a** plucks the string; **i** releases the string immediately after it has been plucked.*

Edition Ricordi   Sy. 2885   © 2012 by G. Ricordi & Co.

INHALT / INDEX

* Serendipity:
Eine zufällige glückliche Entdeckung oder die Fähigkeit etwas per Zufall zu entdecken
A happy discovery by accident or the ability to discover something by accident